Gastric Sleeve Cookbook 2019-2020

The Complete Gastric Sleeve Guide with the Bariatric-Friendly and Healthy Recipes for Every Stage of Bariatric Surgery Recovery

By
Ashley Evans

Table of Content

Introduction

Unlike my peers, I was a fat child with a passion for food. No matter how much I did physical activities, I used to regain because I would replenish what I lost by eating extra. I was a food coinsure since childhood and loved good food. As a result, fight against obese, and weight control was a part of my life, which I could never win. My weight used to fluctuate during my teenagers. But after I decided to become a professional chef and started my training in that direction, I lost control over my weight completely.

As I progressed in my career with my passion for cooking and making people happy with culinary delights, my weight continued to rise. Another reason for my weight gain was that I was detected with hypothyroidism at an early age of 30. This condition of mine called for strict diet control and maintenance of a healthy lifestyle, none of which was happening owning to my hectic work schedule and non-adherence to any dietary restrictions.

My weight was rising, and as a result, I started developing problems like high blood pressure and a high level of blood sugar. Losing weight was essential for my survival. I started feeling fatigued, lacked the enthusiasm that everyone was once envious of and slowly depression crept into my personality.

I struggled with depression for five long years with medication and counseling supporting my recovery. During this phase of my life, it became clear to me that a healthy body can only carry a healthy mind. A body that is unfit and plagued with different medical conditions cannot support a healthy mind. They are connected.

Beginning of my weight loss journey starts from here, with determination, patience, and perseverance. After a few months of dieting and exercising, I began feeling better. But my physician warned me of any heavy exercises or rigorous training sessions, which was contrary to the instructions I had from my gym trainer for shedding excess fat. My physician asked me strictly not to go for such regimes because my health condition would not support that. He informed me about sleeve gastrectomy as an alternative way to weight loss.

My research on the subject prompted me to have a lot of awareness, especially after post-operation care, food practices, diet control, and exercises, which is imperative to accomplish the surgery objectives.

After reading various research articles, I could find the surgery is a major one, and even though it is one of the safest and successful preferred treatment for obese, it also has a lot of drawbacks. The drawbacks can cover by strict diet control. For making you healthy and lead a normal life, I have developed this cookbook, with a lot of emphasis on quality food.

Before you decided to go for sleeve, it is imperative to have a reasonable understanding of the bariatric surgery, post-operation care, diet, and exercise. The book will give you some vital information on the various type of sleeve gastrectomy and diet regime.

Part I

Chapter 1 Sleeve Gastrectomy

Sleeve gastrectomy was new information for me, and I was skeptical about the success of the surgery. Then, I put a lot of effort to study the subject and collected a lot of information. It is a surgical weight-loss procedure, and after undergoing the treatment, the patient can accomplish weight loss objectives by reducing food consumption as recommended by the dietitian.

During the process, the surgeon removes 75 percent of the stomach along the greater curvature permanently by laparoscopic surgery. After the surgery, the stomach looks like a sleeve and can hold only a small portion of food than what was consuming previously. Previously the surgery used to carry out on super obese people, but presently it has been commonly performing on patients as part of weight loss treatment with BMI more than 40.

The concept behind the surgery is to limit the intake of food. When the size of the stomach reduced surgically, the stomach cannot accommodate more food. Such restriction will help to reduce consumption and can help to reduce weight. Further to this, the procedure will push the body for some hormonal changes that can induce weight loss.

Various studies on the sleeve gastrectomy show a result of about 60% of the total excess weight, and a patient can get a better result by adopting strict diet control and recommended exercises if carried out religiously.

On my research, I have realized that, during sleeve gastrectomy, the patients don't have to undergo any implantation. Which means, no foreign body implantation in your body. Further, the process doesn't demand any complex rearrangements of intestines, which is a common process while undergoing a gastric bypass.

One of the positive parts of this bariatric surgery is that patients can eat most of the food items after the surgery recovery period, including vegetables and meats. Since it is not like a gastric bypass or adjustable gastric band procedure, you have to live with the new body condition, as it is permanent and a rollback is impossible.

My Bold Decision

After considering its pros and cons, I decided to go for sleeve gastrectomy. The procedure took an hour or so to complete, and I had to spend two nights in the hospital. I began walking the day after the surgery with some pain around the incisions. I used to depend on pain-relieving medicines, and the pain subsidized in a few days. I was advised to take rest for a week or so and return to work after that. My doctor strictly instructed not to lift anything heavy for a month. Also, I had to go for regular follow-up checkups.

The result was surprising. I lost weight significantly in subsequent months and regained the shape of my body. My medical conditions were under control. However, one issue that I began facing was the type of food I could eat. My truncated stomach could not bear all those food items that I used to love eating. I had to restrict my diet to a typical type of eating that is blunt, low in spices, and carbs. I had to alter my food habit and way to lead my life. This change helped me lose weight further.

People were amazed to see my transformation. I was happy and satisfied with the way my life was progressing, with one small discomfort. I began experimenting and figured out a few recipes and techniques that can serve both the purposes.

As I used to go for follow-up checkups, I met many other fellow patients, and we shared our post-operation experience to find that all are suffering from the same problem. Our main concern was what to eat and what should be the right portion? How can we cook the food with rich nutritional values, keeping the volume less? Some of them sought my advice as I am a chef.

What Will Happen to Your Body After The Bariatric Surgery?

We have already discussed the procedure of sleeve gastrectomy. When a portion of the stomach gets removed, there will be a considerable level of reduction in the secretion of ghrelin hormone. It is responsible for generating hunger, hence is known as the 'hunger hormone.' Because of the slow secretion of the ghrelin hormone, the patient underwent bariatric surgery will feel less hunger.

The hormone also plays an important role in blood sugar metabolism. As a result, type 2 diabetes patient can reduce the dependence on medication. Apart from the benefits, it also has some disadvantages, which I will discuss in the latter part of the content.

When Can a Patient opt For Sleeve Gastrectomy?

The surgical option can apply to patients, who have tried all weight loss options such as exercise and diet control. Further, the following are also the conditions considered for bariatric surgery.

- The patient must be in extreme obese stage.
- The body mass index (BMI) should be more than 40 or higher.
- Some patients with a BMI of 35-39.9 and suffering from type 2 diabetes, other weight-related health issues, chronic sleep apnea, or high blood pressure.
- Sometimes the surgery also recommended for patients with a BMI of 30-34 but suffering from acute health issues due to obese.

What Is the Use Of Performing Sleeve Gastrectomy?

It is a proven successful solution for a patient suffering from life-threatening obese issues, and it helps to reduce weight. The surgery is a relief for a patient with the following conditions.

- High blood pressure
- High cholesterol
- Type 2 diabetes
- Infertility
- Heart alignments
- Gastroesophageal reflux disease
- Obstructive sleep apnea

6

Different Types Of Bariatric Surgery

There Are Five Types Of Bariatric Surgeries:

- Roux-en-Y Gastric Bypass
- Sleeve Gastrectomy
- Duodenal Switch
- Revisional Surgery
- Laparoscopic Adjustable Gastric Banding

Roux-en-Y Gastric Bypass

This procedure splits the stomach into two sections surgically. The small upper part of the stomach surgically linked to the esophagus, which continues to receive food as usual, while the lower portion tinkered to dissociate from the food. The small intestine receives food directly from the newly created small stomach.

Sleeve Gastrectomy

In this process, 75 percent of stomach removed vertically, leaving a sleeve type portion for receiving food.   During the dissection process, a considerable part of the stomach that produces ghrelin hormone, which is responsible for hunger feeling also get removed. The remaining portion will be producing less amount of hunger hormone; hence, the patient will feel less hunger.

As the nerves to the stomach and the valve leading from the stomach to the small intestine remain unchanged, this procedure preserves the functions of the stomach yet considerably reduces the volume. The small intestine remains unaffected.

Duodenal Switch

Duodenal switch has two phases. In stage 1, the surgeon first performs a vertical sleeve gastrectomy procedure. After 12-18 months of the first surgery, the surgeon performs biliopancreatic diversion with duodenal switch. This process connects the remaining part of the stomach to the lower portion of the small intestine, causing significant malabsorption of calories and nutrients.

Revisional Surgery

Revisional procedures supplements and correct can maximizes the effectiveness of past surgery.

Laparoscopic Adjustable Gastric Banding

A silicone elastic ring is placed surgically around the upper part of the stomach. The ring is then inflated with saline solution to tighten the opening from the upper abdomen to the lower belly so that the band decreases hunger and makes the patient eat less and still feel satisfied.

Preparations for Gastric Sleeve Bariatric Surgery

If you are planning for the bariatric surgery, doing a physical checkup will make sure whether the body is healthy to prepare for the procedure. But physical health is not the only requirement; a sound emotional state is also vital for a successful surgery and weight loss to follow.

Lifestyle Alterations:

You must keep in mind that the real treatment doesn't begin or end with the gastric sleeve, and that is why it is critical for patients to start making changes before the surgery. Consult with your medical care team to get the right guidelines on lifestyle and behavioral alterations during the preparation of the surgery, which can even take months or up to a year.

During the time of preparation, the surgeon will devise the right diet plan by considering the age, health conditions, weight, and other characteristics of patients. Adopting healthy life habits and lifestyle changes increase the chance of losing more weight after the sleeve gastrostomy.

Start with Realistic Expectations

Do not expect yourself to wake up thin after bariatric surgery. In fact, you might weight more while leaving the hospital due to the accumulated fluid. Remember that the surgery is not an immediate answer to weight loss, but it is an internal tool in the form of a smaller stomach which helps you on your weight loss journey in the future.

It takes another six months to lose half of your excess weight. After that, it might take another year to reach your weight loss goal. Understand that your weight loss journey will take some time and of course, a lot of effort. Having a well-designed idea of the whole process will help you stay on track.

Confront a Food Addiction

If you are a food addict, then ensure that you address it before surgery. Having a small stomach trough bariatric surgery is not going to make things perfect; you need to control your eating patterns and emotional needs. These days, many people use food to battle daily stress.

But this is not the best way to manage our problem and can create further issues down the road. You must be at a point when you recognize and confront any food addiction to change and feel better. Focus on your long-term goals and learn to manage food to maintain your weight loss goals. Make sure that your food intake is sharply restricted primarily for the first few months. Also, eat food slowly so that it takes at least 20 minutes to finish your small meals. Stop grazing junk food to lose more pounds effectively

Recovery After the Surgery

Any typical patient can return to work after 2-3 weeks of surgery if your job involves only mild activities. However, you won't be able to get back to the full range of activities, especially to a strenuous exercise routine for about 4-6 weeks after surgery.

Once the recovery phase is over, you can start with light exercise to maximize the long-term success of the procedure and enhance your weight loss. During the initial phases of recovery, you must take a limited quantity and type of food. To start

with, you can only have the fluid kind of foods, and over the weeks, you can gradually have regular diets subject the doctor's advice.

Tips to Prepare Before the Surgery

- ➤ Learn about weight loss surgery
- ➤ Quit smoking and discontinue the use of tobacco
- ➤ Make healthy changes in your diet
- ➤ Start tracking food and water intake
- ➤ Begin a disciplined exercise routine
- ➤ Commit not to gain additional weight
- ➤ Change emotional dependence on food
- ➤ Focus on your mental and emotional health

The Pros and Cons Of Sleeve Gastrectomy

Sleeve Gastrectomy is a surgical procedure for weight loss treatment. In this process, a large portion of the stomach surgically removes vertically and makes it smaller in size than the original one. The new sleeve-shaped stomach will be narrow in shape something similar like a banana, which can accommodate only a small portion of the food and you do not feel hungry even after eating a small amount of food.

The sleeve gastrectomy is laparoscopic surgery. The laparoscope is a camera mounted surgical tool, by which the surgeon can see the patient's inside portion of the belly. It helps the surgeon to operate precisely. As the surgery involves the use of a laparoscope, it is known as laparoscopy.

As it is a surgical procedure, the patient undergoes anesthesia before the operation. Anesthesia is mainly in the form of an injection, keep the patient asleep during the procedure, and also makes the complete process painless.

Once the surgeon removes the major portion of the stomach, the hormone responsible for making you feel hungry also gets removed. Which ultimately makes the patient feel less hungry even after taking a small diet.

Drawbacks:

Before we jump on the surgical procedure, you should know the risk of the procedure. Sleeve Gastrectomy increases the risk of having gallstones. To protect the patients

from this situation, the surgeons generally recommend removing the gallbladder. Most of the time, the removal of gallbladder executed along with the sleeve gastronomic procedure.

While in some cases doctors also recommend the patients to get it removed before the main procedure. Along with this, a patient should know that it is an irreversible procedure, which means once it has done, it cannot reverse.

Surgery Procedure:

- During the procedure, the surgeon shall make 3 to 5 small incisions in the patient's belly.

- The incisions are for putting the surgical tools and instruments inside the belly.

- Along with the other tools and instruments, the surgeon also passes a small camera, which helps to have clear internal visibility. This camera is called a laparoscope.

- Next, the surgeon passes some gas inside the stomach. This gas is entirely harmless to the human body. The gas ultimately helps in the expansion of the belly and makes the area ready for surgery.

- Once all preoperational conditions met, the surgeon vertically removes a large portion of the stomach.

- After the surgery, the patient will get a long banana-shaped stomach, which is a lot smaller in size as compared to the earlier one.

- The best part of the surgery is, it doesn't involve any long cut in your muscles responsible for the passage of food.

- Once the process is over, the surgeon shall remove all the instruments and close the incisions with stitches.

All the steps mentioned above in the Sleeve Gastrectomy will take about 60 to 90 minutes to complete.

Why Should You Get Sleeved?

If you are the one who is extremely obese and not able to reduce weight with dieting, exercise, and other routines, then you are left no option other than Sleeve Gastrectomy.

Sleeve Gastrectomy is a major surgery which involves a lot of post-surgery care. After the operation, the patient needs to take proper care of the diet and other activities. You should know how to control your diet and follow the guidelines because, if a patient fails to follow the post-operation recommendation, the result won't be satisfactory to the expectations and also chances are there to develop other health-related complications.

A Patient Can Undergo Sleeve Gastrectomy If:

- If your Body Mass Index (BMI) is 40 and above, then the doctor may advise for the Sleeve Gastrectomy, provided if all other options could not yield a positive result.
- Average BMI of a healthy person is about 18.5 and 25. The weight and height of the person are what gives a proper BMI. (BMI=weight in kg divided by the square of the height in meters) The surgery will make your BMI just as required by reducing hunger and ultimately reducing the weight.
- Also, if a person has a BMI of 35 and above along with the conditions which can likely lead to heart disease, type 2 diabetes and obstructive sleep apnea, the

doctor can recommend you to go for the Sleeve Gastrectomy. It will eventually reduce the risk of the mentioned, chronic weight-related conditions.

- The Sleeve Gastrectomy can reduce around 85% area of the stomach by making the capacity for 2 to 5 oz. of food.
- The patient required a few months to recover from the surgery, and after the recovery period, the patient can control eating habits lifelong.
- If a patient is too heavy to reduce weight and there are no other options left with, then the doctor may advise going for the surgery. Patients with a heavy body would find it challenging to adopt the recommended weight loss exercises, and as a solution, the surgeon may suggest Sleeve Gastrectomy to reduce the obese condition.
- A doctor can also suggest this surgery if the patient has tried all other methods and still not able to reduce the weight. The sleeve surgery will reduce the hunger causing hormones and making you eat less because a large portion of the hunger producing hormone section also will get dissected and removed.
- Sleeve Gastrectomy doesn't have many risks, or we can say that it just has general surgery risks. That is why doctors are giving preference to this procedure. However, the surgery includes risk of gastritis, vomiting due to overeating, stomach, and intestinal injury.
- As the procedure is irreversible, doctors always give preference to all the other methods before proceeding with sleeve gastrectomy.

These are the reasons why one should get Sleeve Gastrectomy done.

Chapter 2 Gastric Sleeve Diet

Starting over the food

Post Sleeve Gastrectomy Diet helps the patient to start over the food intake all over again once done with the procedure successfully. The diet is specially designed to let the stomach heal after the procedure and to create a weight-loss pattern. A doctor or dietitian can guide you exactly how to follow the new diet practice, the timing of food consumption and what foods to avoid, etc. Following the new diet instructions will help you to reduce weight in the best possible way.

The new diet plan will not just help you reduce weight but will also make you practice the habit of eating less amount of food. Starting over the food in the recommended manner will keep the patient away from complications and possible side effects of the surgery.

Individual Diet Details:

As the body is different from one another, the diet also will have to plan according to the body condition and metabolic activities. Getting back to solid food required a well-organized approach, which every patient has to follow religiously. However, all of this also depends on how fast your body accepts the new eating patterns and how fast the body can heal from the surgery.

Doctors generally advise patients to get back to the regular food after completing three months of the post-surgery diet course suggested by the dietitian.

Points To Be Considered While Starting Over The Food:

- Keep some time gap between eating and drinking, as if not done correctly, it can create dumping syndrome. This syndrome occurs due to the frequent passage of food and liquid through the small intestine.
- Eating food too often can also cause vomiting, sweating, nausea, dizziness, and diarrhea.
- To avoid dehydration post-surgery, one has to drink at least 2 liters of fluid every day.
- Eat food, which is higher in protein.
- Do not take liquid with meals. There should be a break of at least

30 minutes between food and fluid intake.

- The consumption of alcohol is strictly prohibited.
- One should never forget to take vitamins and mineral supplements as directed by the doctor.
- Avoid eating food, fruits, and drinks with a higher level of sugar and fat.
- Once you have started taking a solid diet, you should chew food till you get the consistency of the puree.
- Excess intake of caffeine can cause dehydration; hence limit its consumption.

What You Can Eat Or Drink While Starting Over The Food:

The cookbook gives a general idea about the foods you can eat or drink while starting over the food. I have applied a conscious effort to get the best result, after having thorough research on the subject, that can help every sleeved individual like me to lead an easy life. The following categories of food are the best option while adopting a new diet plan.

- **Liquid**: First few days post-surgery, you may take liquids only. Here you can go with, unsweetened juice, skimmed milk, decaffeinated coffee or tea, sugar-free gelatin, broth, and popsicles.
- **Pureed food**: Around a week after the procedure, you will be able to eat pureed food. Here, your food should be in the form of a smooth paste. You can have about 4 to 6 small meals in a day. You can pick your food from soft scrambled eggs, soft fruits and cooked vegetables, lean ground meat, poultry or fish, strained cream soups, cooked cereal, and cottage cheese. Add skim milk, broth, juice, or water to give you the right consistency.
- **Soft foods**: After a few weeks of pureed food diet, you can start having soft foods. You can pick from Flaked fish, Cottage cheese, soft and seedless fruits, Ground lean meat, rice, and egg. Have it 4 to 5 times a day and in the form of small meals.
- **Solid food:** Check with your doctor before consuming solid food. You can go with carbonated drinks, cooked fibrous vegetables, red meat, spicy foods, popcorn, bread, raw vegetables, nuts and seeds, fried foods.

Embracing Eating Without Fear After Gastric Sleeve

The decision to undergo gastric sleeve surgery is a major operation, and it creates a permanent change on your stomach, as a large portion of the stomach removed through surgery. Surgery is just a tool, but the true lasting weight loss happens when you choose to adopt good habits and abandon bad ones. So, I recommend you to eat right after the surgery as follows. The following tips have helped me to reap the weight-loss objective and hope you too can accomplish your dreams.

Choose Foods Suggested By Your Dietician

Stick on to the basic principles of the bariatric diet and try sticking on to the do's and don'ts as you can. In the beginning, stick on to the rules and continue it for several weeks. Develop the ability to control your urge, so that gradually you can get on track.

Stop Eating At The First Sign Of Fullness

When you feel you are about to get full, stop right there. To be mindful of your fullness, eat slowly. If you eat fast, it makes you unable to notice when you get full. Take half an hour to finish your meals and half an hour to one hour before and after each meal to drink water or any liquid.

The new opening made through surgery from your stomach to small intestine is quite narrow, and it can get blocked by large chunks of food. Have small bites of food and thoroughly chew it to puree well before swallowing.

Keep Away From Food High In Fat And Sugar

Foods rich in sugar and fat can travel quickly, and these can have a negative effect on your weight loss also. If too much sugar or fat-rich food goes to your small intestine in a fast way, you will experience nausea or vomiting after meals, which is commonly called dumping syndrome.

Keep Your Blood Sugar Stable

Stable blood keeps your hunger pangs stable, which means no mood swings. To control your blood sugar level- avoid simple carbohydrates including white bread, white rice, potatoes, and anything rich with sugar like ice-cream, donuts, and candy. Make sure that you consume good carbs in right portions with a high amount of proteins. Include brown foods like brown rice, whole grain bread, vegetables, apples, and fruits loaded with fiber to keep yourself full and regulate your bowel movements.

Learn From Your Mistake

Understand that it is common for all patients to make mistakes after the surgery. We are all human and have unique imperfections. Making mistakes doesn't make you a bad person but make sure that you learn from them. Commit to yourself so that you don't go back to old you and make dietary mistakes as you did earlier. Rely on medical professionals or friends and family when you feel like you need support.

Be Mindful When Eating Out

Whenever you eat out make sure that you ask for what you need. Keep in mind that when you get out, you are not just paying for the meal but the service also. Ask your server questions to know about what goes into your meal and how has it prepared. Let them know that you are on a strict diet. Order ala carte and watch out your portions. Even if you want to indulge a bit, go ahead but make sure that you stop at just a bite or two.

Controlling Food Craving after Gastric Sleeve

Food craving can pose a challenge in your after bariatric surgery. Cravings can be a result of pressure, stress, boredom, not following a proper schedule or other reasons. It is brain chemistry and nothing to do with nutrients. The craving centers on texture, creamy or crunchy or even taste, sweet and salty. But they have something in common- overindulgence and sabotage on your weight loss efforts.

Tips To Prevent Potential Food Cravings

Don't Skip Meals

If you skip an already planned snack or meal, you are putting yourself at risk of getting extreme hunger pangs later. With hunger comes craving and urge to eat unhealthy food. Give your body proper food before you lose control.

Resist Sweets

I know, resisting sweets doesn't come easy. Rather than depriving yourself until you crave, you can indulge in a little with small servings. If you crave for chocolate, have a small piece of dark chocolate. However, be careful to avoid processed sugar and candies as it comes with a lot of calories and fat content.

Divert Your Focus

When you crave for a particular food, divert your concentration on something other than food. Try doing things you like, indulge in another activity, read a book, or talk to a friend. Don't force yourself not to think about your craving as that will cause to stick on to that particular thing even more. Get your mind off from that and do something else; you can even go for a walk.

Remind Your Goals

This one is pretty difficult, I understand. Bariatric surgery is a big decision you have taken after going through a lot of research and understanding. You already know your goals, but sometimes you need to remember the things you already know. Have a look into an old picture of yours if it matches your weight loss goals or reminds yourself how far you have come. Ask yourself whether giving in to your temporary craving will help or hinder the process you have made till now.

Drink Water

Whenever you feel like craving strikes in, grab a glass of water to make sure that what you crave for is water and not just anything else. Sometimes, dehydration can cause cravings and leads to grazing and overeating. Heavily hydrated people often experience fewer cravings, and you feel better throughout the day.

Demonstrate Self Compassion

If you want to kick-start your weight loss journey at a faster pace, first you have to cut the mental fat-which leads to cutting off the waistline fat. When trying to improve lifestyle and diet, most people do find until some interference happen-like work pressure, family problems, relationship issues, or something else. In that scenario, you ensure that you keep the momentum to continue your journey.

You are indeed on a tough mission, and it's not okay to give up. But some people emphasize more on this and pressurize them hindering weight loss again due to stress. Some even go overboard by reducing portion too much, skipping meals and punishing their body by thinking that less food intake leads to weight loss.

Here are some tips and tricks to keep with your weight loss journey while developing a deep self-compassion.

Set Realistic Goals And Expectations

When setting realistic goals, you also have to include cheat days giving room for a slight indulgence. For many, goals are unrealistic and hard to stick with, which leads to mental stress when they are not able to follow it.

Get Help When Needed

It is common for people who undergo bariatric surgery to crave for mental support at any phase before or after the surgery. If you feel like you need help or counseling after the surgery, get this done or else it can even lead to mental stress and depression.

Navigating Fear

As you have done the weight loss surgery, you might be experiencing a sort of relief as you have made a significant step accounting to your weight loss journey. But along with relief, comes worry. Worry about whether bowel obstruction or dumping syndrome could happen or what if you don't get the weight off post-surgery.

All you have to do is to give yourself time to get used to your new body. Stay committed to your lifestyle changes, and if you hit a weight loss plateau, you can talk to your doctor. There are dietary changes and workout that can help you overcome the plateau. It is not easy, but never impossible.

Best Way to Eat Out

Since you have undergone sleeve gastrectomy, never feel like eating an ordinary person. You have to always keep in mind that you are on a personal journey. Your friends and family may order unrestricted foods, even junk foods. Never allow that deter you or regret choosing healthy. But that doesn't mean that you can't dine out after gastric sleeve. Follow these tips to dine out after bariatric surgery.

Substitute side dishes

Instead of ordering customary mashed potato or French fries along with your meal; ask for a salad or a serving of steamed vegetables. Most restaurants offer customized substitutions at no or a minimal additional cost. Ask for all sauces and dressings to be served on the side.

Know how the food prepared

The biggest challenge of dining out after your weight loss surgery is that you don't know what goes into your diet. But you can always check with the restaurant staff to gain knowledge about preparation methods and ingredients. Another great way is to choose foods wisely from baked, roasted, steamed, grilled, or poached instead of fried items.

Ask for a to-go-container

No problem if the restaurant serves on a full-sized entree, you can always ask for a to-go container to pack your remaining meal away for later so that you won't be forced to clean your plate.

Look for a light menu

Restaurants prepare food in big portions for a large number of people, and the amount of oil goes into each dish is 2 or 4 times what we use at home. The best way is to look for a light menu prepared without extra oil or butter.

Choose your adult beverage wisely

You can indulge in drinks once in a while if you have got hold of its portion. Whenever you want to order an adult beverage, try a glass of red wine as low-calorie alternatives to mixed drinks and heavy beers. These strategies will help you enjoy your next dining out experience. Again, remember, it is best to limit everything to a moderate level.

Count calories of every meal

It is another important tip that helps you to eat out without guilt. Watch the number of calories you consume when eating out. Most restaurants will provide you with the calorie content of the dishes they serve and also the nutritional facts as well.

Avoid drinking along with your meals

Drinking any liquid with your meals will push the food down fast, and this brings in more foods in your pouch. Hence, it is a best practice to avoid liquids 15 minutes before and 30 minutes after every meal.

Indulgence in fast food

When it comes to fast food, the variety of choices can be endless, but make sure you choose your plate wisely. Get your dressing on the side and dip your fork to dressing instead of adding it directly to your meal. It can save loads of calories.

Part II

Stage 1:   Clear Fluids

Lemon Balm Tea

Preparation Time: 5 Minutes, Cooking Time: 15 Minutes, Servings: 5

Ingredients
- 1 cup lemon balm
- 5 cup water
- 1 tbsp. lemon zest

Instructions:
1. Set water on to boil. Once boiling, add in lemon balm and zest, then remove from heat.
2. Allow to cool.
3. Strain, serve and enjoy.

Nutritional Value Per Serving:
Calories: 13.3, Fat: 0g , Carbs: 3.6g, Protein: 0g

Watermelon sorbet

Preparation Time: 5 Minutes, Servings: 6

Ingredients:

- 4½ cup crushed ice cubes,
- ½ lb. cubed melon
- 1 tbsp. orange zest, grated

Instructions:
1. Place all ingredients in a blender.
2. Blend the ingredients for 30 seconds.
3. Serve immediately.

Nutritional Value Per Serving:
Calories: 231.1, Fat: 0.2g, Carbs: 59.6g, Protein: 0.6g

Ginger Tea

Preparation Time: 5 Minutes, Cooking Time: 10 Minutes, Servings: 2

Ingredients
- 3 tsps. grated gingerroot
- 3 cup boiling water

Instructions:
1. Combine ingredients together and allow to rest, covered for at least 10 minutes.
2. Serve and Enjoy!

Nutritional Value Per Serving:
Calories: 26.8, Fat: 0g, Carbs: 6.8g, Protein: 0.1g

Peanut Tea

Preparation Time: 2 Minutes, Cooking Time: 3 Minutes, Servings: 2

Ingredients
- 5 tbsps. peanuts, ground
- 1 tsp. cinnamon
- 1 cup water

Instructions:
1. Using a saucepan, heat the water, then stir in remaining ingredients.
2. Serve hot.

Nutritional Value Per Serving:
Calories: 40, Fat: 3.58g, Carbs: 1.4g , Protein: 1.51g

Pork Bone Broth

Preparation Time: 20 Minutes, Cooking Time: 2 Hours, Servings: 5

Ingredients

- 1 oz. pork bones
- 2 tbsps. apple cider vinegar
- 1 sliced onion
- 6 garlic cloves
- 1 tbsp. cooking oil
- ½ tsp. salt
- ½ tsp. white pepper
- 1-inch ginger slice
- Water

Instructions:

1. In a large skillet, add bones with water, onion, garlic, ginger, oil, vinegar, salt and pepper, and stir. Cover with lid.
2. Cook for 2 hours on low.
3. Strain the broth and discard residue.
4. Serve hot and enjoy.

Nutritional Value Per Serving:
Calories: 37.7, Fat: 0.2g, Carbs: 8.2g, Protein: 1 g

Red Apple and Carrot Tea

Preparation Time: 5 Minutes, Cooking Time: 5 Minutes, Servings: 3

Ingredients

- 1 cup red apples, peeled, chunks
- 2 sliced carrots
- ½ cup seeded lychee
- 2 cup water

Instructions:

1. Blend apples with carrots, lychee and water.
2. Using a saucepan, mix all the above ingredients and allow to come to a boil.
3. Remove from heat and let rest for about 5 minutes.
4. Strain, serve and enjoy!

Nutritional Value Per Serving:
Calories: 184, Fat: 0g, Carbs: 44.6g, Protein: 1g

Banana Icy Pops

Preparation Time: 30 Minutes, Cooking Time: 4 Hours, Servings: 8

Ingredients:
- 1 cup boiling water
- 1 package Jell-O, fruit-flavored
- 1 banana
- 1 cup plain yogurt

Instructions:
1. Add all the ingredients in a blender. Blend everything until smooth.
2. Pour mixture into a popsicle mold or in a plastic cup.
3. Place in a freezer until hard.
4. Serve and enjoy!

Nutritional Value Per Serving:
Calories: 93, Fat: 0.4g, Carbs: 22g, Protein: 2.2g

Clear Vegetable Stock

Preparation Time: 10 Minutes, Cooking Time: 40 Minutes, Servings: 12

Ingredients
- 1 tbsp. olive oil
- 1 onion
- 2 stalks of celery
- 2 carrots
- 1 bunch chopped green onions
- 8 minced cloves garlic
- 8 sprigs parsley, fresh
- 6 sprigs thyme, fresh
- 2 bay leaves
- 1 tsp. salt
- 2 quarts water

Instructions:
1. Chop scrubbed vegetables into 1-inch chunks.
2. Heat oil in a soup pot. Add onion, celery, carrots, green onions, bay leaves, thyme, parsley and garlic. Cook over high heat 5-10 minutes stirring frequently.
3. Add salt and water and bring to a boil. Simmer for 30 minutes on low.
4. Strain, discard vegetables and enjoy.

Nutritional Value Per Serving:
Calories: 37, Fat: 1.4g, Carbs: 5.9g, Protein: 1.3g

Orange Carrot Tea

Preparation Time: 2 Minutes, Cooking Time: 9 Minutes, Servings:

Ingredients

- 4 halved oranges
- 12 oz. diced carrots
- 4 cup water

Instructions:
1. Pour all ingredients into the Vitamix and secure the lid; or
2. Pour all ingredients into a saucepan and allow to come to a boil.
3. Kill the heat and allow to cool.
4. Strain, serve and enjoy!

Nutritional Value Per Serving:
Calories: 93, Fat: 0.4g , Carbs: 22g, Protein: 2.2g

Peppermint Tea

Preparation Time: 5 Minutes, Cooking Time: 5 Minutes, Servings: 4

Ingredients:
- ½ cup dried Peppermint Leaf
- 4 cup Water, hot

Instructions:
1. Set water on to boil. Once boiling, add in peppermint leaves and remove from heat.
2. Cover and allow to cool for approximately 5 minutes.
3. Strain, serve and enjoy.

Nutritional Value Per Serving:
Calories 34.2, Fat: 0g, Carbs: 9.1g, Protein: 0.1g

Pecan Tea

Preparation Time: 1 Minute, Cooking Time: 4 Minutes, Servings: 2

Ingredients
- 5 tbsps. pecans, ground
- 1 tsp. cinnamon
- 1 cup water

Instructions:
1. In a saucepan, heat the water and then stir in remaining ingredients.
2. Serve hot.

Nutritional Value Per Serving:
Calories: 40, Fat: 3.58g, Carbs: 1.4g, Protein: 1.5g

Almond Tea

Preparation Time: 5 minutes, Cooking Time: 5 minutes, Servings: 4

Ingredients

- 5 tablespoons almond powder
- 1 teaspoon cinnamon
- 1 cup of water

Instructions
1. Take a saucepan and place it over high heat, add water and stir in rest of the ingredients.
2. Bring to a boil and remove heat.
3. Serve and enjoy!

Nutritional Value Per Serving:
Calories: 40, Total Fat: 3g, Saturated Fat: 0g, Protein: 1.5g, Carbs: 1.4g, Fiber: 0.1g

Orange Vanilla Tea

Preparation Time: 10 minutes,
Cooking Time: 5 minutes, Servings: 4

Ingredients

- ¼ cup of water
- 2 oranges, sliced
- ¼ teaspoon vanilla extract

Instructions

1. Take a saucepan and place it over high heat, add all of the mixtures and bring to a boil.
2. Remove heat and let it sit for 5 minutes.
3. Strain the mixture and serve, enjoy!

Nutritional Value Per Serving:
Calories: 60, Total Fat: 1g, Saturated Fat: 0g, Protein: 2g, Carbs: 14g, Fiber: 0.1g

Chicken Bone Broth

Preparation Time: 10 minutes ,
Cooking Time: 2 hours   , Servings: 4
Ingredients:
- 1 ounce of chicken bones
- 2 tablespoons apple cider vinegar
- 1 onion, sliced
- 6 garlic cloves
- 1 tablespoon cooking oil

- ½ teaspoon salt
- ½ teaspoon white pepper
- 1-inch ginger, sliced
- Water

Instructions:

1. Take a large skillet and add bones, water, onion, garlic, oil, ginger, vinegar, salt, pepper and gently stir.
2. Cover with lid and cook on low heat for 2 hours.
3. Strain the broth and discard any residue.
4. Serve hot and enjoy!

Nutritional Value Per Serving:
Calories: 147, Total Fat: 5g, Saturated Fat: 0g , Protein: 10g , Carbs: 9g , Fiber: 0.5g

Kiwi Sorbet

Preparation Time: 5 minutes, Cooking Time: nil, Servings: 4

Ingredients
- 4 and ½ cups crushed ice cubes
- ½ pound kiwi fruit, chopped
- 1 tablespoon orange zest, grated

Instructions:
1. Add listed ingredients to your blender.
2. Blend for 30 seconds.
3. Serve and enjoy!

Nutritional Value Per Serving:
Calories: 105, Total Fat: 0.3g , Saturated Fat: 0g , Protein: 0.6g, Carbs:26g; , Fiber: 0.1g

Stage 2:   Full Liquids

Alcohol-Free Mint Mojito

Preparation Time: 5 minutes, Cooking Time: 30 minutes   , Servings: 4

Ingredients

- 12/2 cup fresh mint leaves
- 1-ounce lime juice
- ½ cup natural sweetener
- 2 cups of water

Instructions

1. Add water and sweetener in a pot and let it boil for 5 minutes until the syrup has thickened.
2. Transfer mint leaves in a glass jar and pours in the syrup.
3. Cover jar and let it steep for 20 minutes.
4. Create a mixture of a tablespoon of the syrup and half a cup of cold water in a glass, add lime juice and mix, serve and enjoy!

Nutritional Value Per Serving:

Calories: 32, Total Fat: 0g , Saturated Fat: 0g, Protein: 0g , Carbs: 3g, Fiber: 1g

Sugar-Free Strawberry Limeade

Preparation Time: 5 minutes, Cooking Time: 30 minutes, Servings: 4

Ingredients

- ½ teaspoon strawberry extract
- 1 and ½ cups cold water
- Juice of ½ a lime

Instructions:

1. Mix in strawberry extract, lime juice and water in a bowl.
2. Take a cup and add ice cubes, pour the strawberry mixture and enjoy!

Nutritional Value Per Serving:

Calories: 12 , Total Fat: 0g , Saturated Fat: 0g , Protein: 1g , Carbs: 2.1g, Fiber: 0.5g

Hearty Mint Tea

Preparation Time: 5 minutes, Cooking Time: 30 minutes, Servings: 4

Ingredients
- 1-gallon boiling water
- 2 tablespoons mint
- 1 lemon, sliced
- 6 Rooibos tea bags

Instructions:
1. Place water over high heat and let it start boiling.
2. Remove heat and add tea bags.
3. Pour the mixture into a pitcher (alongside teabags, mint and sliced lemon) and let it steep for 30 minutes.
4. Serve and enjoy!

Nutritional Value Per Serving:
Calories: 4 , Total Fat: 0g , Saturated Fat: 0g, Protein: 0.1g, Carbs: 1.4g , Fiber: 0.1g

Orange and Apricot Juice

Preparation Time: 10 minutes, Cooking Time: nil , Servings: 2

Ingredients:
- 2 large oranges, peeled
- 2 large apricots, pitted
- 1 cup pomegranate seeds
- 1 cup of green grapes
- 1 large lemon, peeled
- 1 small ginger slice, peeled

Instructions:
1. Peel oranges and divide them into wedges.
2. Keep it on the side.
3. Wash apricots and cut them in half, remove pits and cut them into small pieces.
4. Cut the top of pomegranate fruit using a sharp knife and slice down each of the white membranes inside the fruit.
5. Pop seeds into a measuring cup and keep it on the side.
6. Peel lemon and cut it lengthwise in half and keep it on the side.
7. Peel ginger slices and keep it on the side.
8. Add orange, apricots, pomegranate, lemon ginger to a juicer and process until well juiced.
9. Chill for 20 minutes and enjoy!

Nutritional Value Per Serving:
Calories: 196, Total Fat: 0.8g , Saturated Fat: 0g, Protein: 4g, Carbs: 48g , Fiber: 6.9g

Apple and Citrus Juice

Preparation Time: 10 minutes, Cooking Time: nil , Servings: 2

Ingredients:

- 1 cup avocado, pitted and chopped
- 1 large cucumber, sliced
- 1 large lemon, peeled
- 1 cup fresh spinach, torn
- 1 large lime, peeled
- 1 small ginger knob, peeled
- 3 ounces of water

Instructions:

1. Peel your avocado and cut it in half. Remove pit and chop the avocado into chunks.
2. Wash cucumber and cut it into thick slices.
3. Keep it on the side.
4. Peel lemon and lime, cut it length in half.
5. Wash your spinach thoroughly and tear it into small parts.
6. Take your juicer and add avocado, cucumber, lemon, lime, spinach, ginger, and process until finely juiced.
7. Let it chill for 20 minutes, serve and enjoy!

Nutritional Value Per Serving:
Calories: 197 , Total Fat: 14g, Saturated Fat: 3g, Protein: 3g , Carbs: 19g , Fiber: 8g

Blueberry Cacao Blast

Preparation Time: 2 Minutes, Cooking Time: 3 Minutes, Servings: 1

Ingredients:

- 1 cup blueberries
- 1 tbsp. raw cacao nibs
- 1 tbsp. chia seeds
- 1 dash cinnamon
- ½ cup chopped spinach
- ½ cup chopped bananas
- 1½ cup almond milk
- 2 scoops whey protein powder

Instructions:

1. Place raspberries, cacao nibs, chia seeds and cinnamon in a blender.
2. Add enough almond milk to reach the max line.
3. Process for 30 seconds or until you get a smooth mixture.
4. Serve immediately in a tall chilled glass.

Nutritional Value Per Serving:
Calories: 321, Carbs: 69.4g, Fat: 2.7g , Protein: 24.7g

Cucumber and Avocado Dill Smoothie

Preparation Time: 2 Minutes, Cooking Time: 3 Minutes, Servings: 2

Ingredients:

- 1 sliced cucumber
- 2 tbsps. chopped dill
- 2 tbsps. lemon juice
- 1 pitted avocado
- 1 c. coconut milk
- 1 tsp. shredded coconut
- 2 sliced kiwi fruit

Instructions:

1. Mix and blend all the above ingredients using a blender.
2. Drain the extract and discard residue.
3. Serve and enjoy.

Nutritional Value Per Serving:
Calories: 165, Fat: 5.5g, Carbs: 24.8g , Protein: 2.3g

Spinach Green Smoothie

Preparation Time:, Cooking Time:, Servings: 2

Ingredients:

- 1 cup baby spinach leaves
- 3 mint leave
- 1 cup 100% grapes juice
- 1 cup 100% pineapple juice
- 2 tbsps. lime juice
- 2 scoops protein powder

Instructions:

1. In a blender add ingredients and blend well 'til puree.
2. Transfer to serving glasses.
3. Serve and enjoy.

Nutritional Value Per Serving:
Calories: 268 ,Fat: 5.5g , Carbs: 11.4g , Protein: 24.3g

Coco - Banana Milkshake

Preparation Time: 2 Minutes, Cooking Time: 3 Minutes, Servings: 1

Ingredients:
- 1 cup coconut milk
- 2 ripe bananas
- 2 tbsps. cinnamon
- ¼ tsp. cardamom powder
- 2 scoops protein powder
- 7 ice cubes

Instructions:
1. In a blender add coconut milk with cardamom powder, cinnamon, bananas and blend well.
2. Pour into glass and add ice chunks.
3. Serve and enjoy.

Nutritional Value Per Serving:
Calories: 191.9, Fat: 7.1g, Carbs: 35.8g, Protein: 25.7g

Strawberry and Cherry Shake

Preparation Time: 2 Minutes, Cooking Time: 3 Minutes, Servings: 2

Ingredients:
- 1 cup strawberries
- 1 cup cherries
- 1 cup almond milk
- ½ cup coconut milk
- 2 scoops protein powder
- A few ice chunks

Instructions:
1. Place all the ingredients in a blender and process well.
2. Serve and enjoy.

Nutritional Value Per Serving:
Calories: 138, Fat: 0g, Carbs: 30g , Protein: 20g

Chia Blueberry Banana Oatmeal Smoothie

Preparation Time: 3 Minutes, Cooking Time: 7 Minutes, Servings: 1
Ingredients:
- 1 cup soy milk
- 1 sliced frozen banana
- ¼ cup frozen blueberries
- ¼ cup oats
- 1 tsp. vanilla extract
- 1 tsp. cinnamon
- 1 tbsp. chia seed

Instructions:
1. Use a blender to mix and blend until the ingredients are combined and smooth.
2. Serve and enjoy!

Nutritional Value Per Serving:
Calories: 178, Fat: 4.2g, Carbs: 36.2g , Protein: 3.2g

Banana-Cherry Smoothie

Preparation Time: 2 Minutes, Cooking Time: 3 Minutes, Servings: 1
Ingredients:
- 1 banana
- 1 cup pitted cherries
- ¼ tsp. nutmeg
- 1scoop protein powder
- 1 cup almond milk

Instructions:
1. Place all ingredients in a blender.
2. Process ingredients until smooth, for 20 seconds.
3. Serve immediately.

Nutritional Value Per Serving:
Calories: 398 , Fat: 2g, Carbs: 89.2g, Protein: 17g

Mango Smoothie

Preparation Time: 2 Minutes, Cooking Time: 3 Minutes, Servings: 2

Ingredients:

- 2 mangos (seeded, diced, frozen)
- 1 cup milk
- ½ cup crushed ice
- 1 cup plain yogurt
- 2 scoops protein powder

Instructions:

1. Combine all ingredients in Vitamix.
2. Process for 30 seconds or until smooth.
3. Serve immediately in a tall glass.

Nutritional Value Per Serving:
Calories: 320, Fat: 0g, Carbs: 8g, Protein: 21g

Cashew Milk

Preparation Time: 2 Minutes, Cooking Time: 3 Minutes, Servings: 5

Ingredients:

- 1 cup-soaked cashew
- 4 cup water
- 3 dates

Instructions:

1. Add all ingredients to Vitamix.
2. Pulse until creamy (should take about 1 min).
3. Enjoy!

Nutritional Value Per Serving:
Calories: 60 , Fat: 2.5g , Carbs: 27.3g, Protein: 8g

Pumpkin and carrot soup

Preparation Time: 3 Minutes, Cooking Time: 22 Minutes, Servings: 4

Ingredients:
- ½ lb. pumpkin puree
- ½ lb. cubed carrots
- 2 cup vegetable stock
- ½ cup chopped onion
- Salt
- Pepper
- 1 tsp. dried thyme
- 2 oz. cauliflower florets
- ½ tbsp. olive oil
- 1 anise star

Instructions:
1. Heat the oil in a pot. Add onion, cauliflower and carrots, and sauté for 15 minutes or until onion is caramelized.
2. Add thyme and stir well.
3. Transfer the vegetables into a Nutri Bullet, add pumpkin puree and vegetable stock, and pulse until smooth.
4. Transfer the mixture into saucepan and simmer, add anise star and simmer over medium-high heat for 5-8 minutes or until heated through.
5. Remove the anise star and discard.
6. Strain and serve immediately.

Nutritional Value Per Serving:
Calories: 70, Fat: 0g , Carbs: 0g , Protein: 2g

Stage 3: Soft Foods Recipes

Easy Baked Tomatoes

Preparation Time: 10 minutes,
Cooking Time: 50 minutes, Servings: 5

Ingredients:

- ¼ cup pine nuts
- Greek seasoning as needed
- ¼ cup low-fat parmesan
- Olive oil spray as needed
- 5-6 whole tomatoes

Ingredients:

1. Pre-heat your oven to 350 degrees F.
2. Slice tomatoes in half lengthwise and transfer to a pan with cut side up.
3. Spray tops of tomato with olive oil spray.
4. Season with pine nuts, cheese, and Greek seasoning.
5. Bake for 50 minutes and serve, enjoy!

Nutritional Value Per Serving:
Calories: 73 , Total Fat: 5g , Saturated Fat: 1g, Protein: 3g , Carbs: 6g , Fiber: 1g

Black Bean Chipotle Hummus

Preparation Time: 5 minutes, Cooking Time: nil, Servings: 4

Ingredients:

- 1 (15 ounces) can, black beans, drained and rinsed
- 1 lime, juiced
- 1 chipotle pepper in adobo sauce
- 1 teaspoon adobo sauce
- 1 teaspoon garlic, minced
- 2 teaspoons ground cumin
- 2 tablespoons extra-virgin olive oil
- ¼ cup fresh cilantro, chopped

Instructions:

1. Take your food processor and add black beans, lime juice, chipotle pepper, adobo sauce, garlic, cumin, olive oil, cilantro and blend on high for 2-3 minutes until smooth.
2. Serve and enjoy!

Nutritional Value Per Serving:
Calories: 52 , Total Fat: 2g , Saturated Fat: 1g , Protein: 2g, Carbs: 6g, Fiber: 1g

Finely Crispy Wok Veggies

Preparation Time: 10 minutes,
Cooking Time: 20 minutes , Servings:
2

Ingredients:

- 1 medium red bell pepper, cut into strips
- 1 medium green bell pepper, cut into strips
- 7-8 pieces baby corn
- ½ cup button mushrooms, canned
- 1 cup cauliflower, chopped into bite-sized pieces
- 1 medium carrot, peeled and cut into strips
- 1 teaspoon oyster sauce
- 1 tablespoon olive oil
- 1 teaspoon salt

Instructions:

1. Wash bell peppers and cut them in half.
2. Remove seeds and cut into strips.
3. Take a large wok pan and heat up olive oil over medium heat, add carrots and cauliflower and cook for 8-10 minutes.
4. Add red and green pepper strips, baby corn, button mushrooms, oyster sauce, cook for 5-7 minutes.
5. Serve veggies with mashed potatoes and sprinkled turmeric.
6. Enjoy!

Nutritional Value Per Serving:

Calories: 236, Total Fat: 6g, Saturated Fat: 0g, Protein: 9g, Carbs: 46g, Fiber: 8g

Cheesy Tomato Omelet

Preparation Time: 5 minutes , Cooking Time: 5-10 minutes, Servings: 4

Ingredients:

- ½ teaspoon butter
- 1 large whole egg
- 1 tablespoon milk
- Salt and pepper to taste
- Garlic powder
- 1 slice cheddar cheese
- 1 tablespoon tomato, chopped

Instructions:

1. Take a 6-inch non-stick skillet and melt butter over medium heat, coat well.
2. Take a small bowl and whisk in egg, milk and pour into skillet.
3. Season with garlic, pepper, salt.
4. Once the edges of the egg mix begin to cook, lift with spatula and tip skillet so uncooked egg flows underneath.
5. Repeat step 3 until top is almost dry. Place cheese slice on top then tomato over half omelet.
6. Once cheese begins to melt, fold in half and serve.

Nutritional Value Per Serving:

Calories: 227 , Total Fat: 19g , Saturated Fat: 2g , Protein: 18g, Carbs: 7g, Fiber: 2g

Stuffed Avocado

Preparation Time: 15 minutes, Cooking Time: 20 minutes, Servings: 4

Ingredients:

- 2 medium-sized ripe avocado, cut in half
- 6 large eggs
- 1 medium tomato, finely chopped
- 3 tablespoons olive oil
- 2 tablespoons fresh parsley, chopped
- 4 tablespoons Greek yogurt
- 1 tablespoon fresh rosemary, chopped
- ½ teaspoon salt
- ¼ teaspoon pepper, ground

Instructions:

1. Pre-heat your oven to 350 degrees F.
2. Take a small baking dish and grease with oil, keep it on the side.
3. Cut avocado in half and scrape out flesh from the center.
4. Take a medium bowl and whisk in eggs, tomatoes, parsley, rosemary, salt, and pepper.
5. Stir until thoroughly incorporated, spoon mixture into avocado shells.
6. Spread stuffed avocado on a baking sheet and bake for 15-20 minutes.
7. Remove and top with yogurt, enjoy!

Nutritional Value Per Serving:

Calories: 385, Total Fat: 35g, Saturated Fat: 5g, Protein: 10g, Carbs: 12g, Fiber: 2g

Best Chocolate Porridge

Preparation Time: 1 minute , Cooking Time: 3 minutes, Servings: 6

Ingredients:
- Small square dark unsweetened chocolate
- 1 tablespoon low-calorie sweetener
- 1 tablespoon chocolate protein powder
- 3 tablespoons porridge oats
- 1 cup skimmed milk

Instructions:
1. Add chocolate, protein powder, milk and oats to a jug.
2. Mix well and transfer to microwave container, cook for 2 minutes.
3. Stir and cook for 20-30 seconds more.
4. Mix in your desired sweetener and spoon mixture into serving bowl.
5. Top with couple blackberries and a bit of chopped chocolate.
6. Enjoy!

Nutritional Value Per Serving:
Calories: 328, Total Fat: 8g , Saturated Fat: 1g, Protein: 23g, Carbs: 41g , Fiber: 10g

Chocolate Chia Pudding

Preparation Time: 10 minutes + 60 minutes to chill, Cooking Time: nil, Servings: 4

Ingredients:
- 2 cups unsweetened soy milk
- 10 drops liquid stevia
- ¼ cup unsweetened cocoa powder
- ¼ teaspoon ground cinnamon
- ¼ teaspoon vanilla extract
- ½ cup chia seeds
- ½ cup fresh raspberries, for garnish

Instructions:
1. Take a small sized bowl and whisk in soy milk, stevia, cocoa powder, cinnamon, vanilla and mix well until combined.
2. Stir in chia seeds.
3. Divide the mixture between 4 small dishes.
4. Cover and let it chill for 1 hour.
5. Once done, garnish with raspberries, enjoy!

Nutritional Value Per Serving:
Calories: 182, Total Fat: 9g, Saturated Fat: 2g , Protein: 11g, Carbs: 14g , Fiber: 14g

Tender Soft Mexican Chicken Salad

Preparation Time: 5 minutes , Cooking Time: 5 minutes , Servings: 5

Ingredients:

- 2 teaspoons juice of jarred salsa
- 1 teaspoon taco seasoning
- 1 tablespoon light mayonnaise
- 1 cup canned chicken, drained

Instructions:

1. Add drained chicken in a bowl and take a fork, break chicken into small pieces.
2. Add mayonnaise to chicken and combine well, mash chicken into mayonnaise with a fork.
3. Add salsa juice and taco seasoning to chicken mix, keep mixing and mash everything well.
4. Serve and enjoy!

Nutritional Value Per Serving:
Calories: 180 , Total Fat: 5g , Saturated Fat: 1g, Protein: 21g, Carbs: 10g, Fiber: 2g

Protein Packed Pumpkin Pie Oatmeal

Preparation Time: 5 minutes, Cooking Time: 5 minutes , Servings: 5

Ingredients:

- 1 cup 1% cottage cheese
- 1 teaspoon Truvia baking blend
- Dash of ginger
- Dash of cloves
- Dash of cinnamon
- ½ cup canned pumpkin
- ½ cup old fashioned oats

Instructions:

1. Add sweetener, spices, pumpkin, and oats in a microwave proof bowl.
2. Cook for 90 seconds on HIGH and stir in cottage cheese.
3. Microwave for 60 seconds more.
4. Let it stand for a minute and enjoy!

Nutritional Value Per Serving:
Calories: 205, Total Fat: 3g, Saturated Fat: 0g , Protein: 14g, Carbs: 34g, Fiber: 6g

Delicious Mugastrone

Preparation Time: 1 minute, Cooking Time: 5 minutes, Servings: 2
Ingredients:
- Salt and pepper to taste
- ¼ ounces dry vermicelli
- 1 and ½ tablespoons frozen mixed vegetables
- 1 tablespoon cooked borlotti beans
- 2/3 cup tomato juice

Instructions:
1. Add tomato sauce to a glass measuring cup, add pepper, salt, noodles, veggies, and beans. Stir well.
2. Transfer to microwave and cook for 2-3 minutes.
3. Top with parmesan and enjoy!

Nutritional Value Per Serving:
Calories: 170, Total Fat: 4g, Saturated Fat: 1g, Protein: 5g , Carbs: 16g, Fiber: 4g

Lemon-Blackberry Frozen Yogurt

Preparation Time: 10 minutes, Cooking Time: nil, Servings: 4
Instructions:
- 4 cups frozen blackberries
- ½ cup low-fat plain Greek yogurt
- 1 lemon, juiced
- 2 teaspoons liquid stevia
- Fresh mint leaves, for garnish

Instructions:
1. Take your food processor and ad blackberries, yogurt, lemon juice, stevia and blend well until smooth.
2. Serve immediately and enjoy with a garnish of fresh mint leaves.

Nutritional Value Per Serving:
Calories: 68, Total Fat: 0g, Saturated Fat: 0g, Protein: 3g , Carbs: 15g , Fiber: 5g

Creamy Cauliflower Dish

Preparation Time: 10 minutes, Cooking Time: 5 minutes, Servings: 5

Ingredients:

- ½ teaspoon pepper
- 4 teaspoon extra virgin olive oil
- ½ teaspoon garlic salt
- 1 teaspoon salted butter
- 1/3 cup low-fat buttermilk
- 3 cloves garlic
- Large head of cauliflower

Instructions:

1. Break your cauliflower into small florets and transfer to a large microwave proof bowl, add garlic and a quarter of water.
2. Microwave for 5 minutes until cauliflower is tender.
3. Use a garlic press and crush garlic cloves, add to food processor and add to cauliflower.
4. Add pepper, garlic salt, butter, two teaspoons olive oil, buttermilk.
5. Process well until creamy and smooth.
6. Drizzle remaining olive oil on top and enjoy!

Nutritional Value Per Serving:
Calories: 113, Total Fat: 6g, Saturated Fat: 2g , Protein: 5g , Carbs: 13g, Fiber: 3g

Beetroot and Butterbean Hummus

- 1-2 cloves garlic, crushed
- 14 ounces butterbeans, drained and rinsed
- 8 ounces cooked beetroot

Instructions:
1. Dice beetroot and cut into small cubes.
2. Add butterbeans in a food processor and season with salt, pepper, yogurt, oil, chives, and garlic.
3. Blitz until the mixture is a nice puree.
4. Fold in diced beetroot and blitz gently.
5. Serve and enjoy!

Nutritional Value Per Serving:
Calories: 80 , Total Fat: 2g , Saturated Fat: 0g , Protein: 4.2g, Carbs: 10g, Fiber: 0.5g

Preparation Time: 5 minutes, Cooking Time: nil, Servings: 4

Ingredients:
- Salt and pepper as needed
- 1 tablespoon extra-virgin olive oil
- 2 tablespoons Fat-Free Greek yogurt
- Bunch of chives, chopped

Raisin and Oats Mug Cakes

- 1/16 teaspoon salt
- ½ tablespoons canola oil
- 1/8 teaspoons baking soda
- 1/8 teaspoons vanilla extract
- 1/8 teaspoons hazelnut extract
- ¾ tablespoons oats
- 1 teaspoon lemon juice
- ¼ teaspoon baking powder

Instructions:
1. Whisk in all ingredients in a microwave-proof mug and cook on high for 1 minute.
2. Let it cool, serve and enjoy!

Nutritional Value Per Serving:
Calories: 185, Total Fat: 1.7g , Saturated Fat: 1g, Protein: 8g, Carbs: 39g , Fiber: 10g

Preparation Time: 10 minutes ,
Cooking Time: 1 minute, Servings: 3

Ingredients:
- 1 and ½ tablespoons flour
- 1 and ½ tablespoons almond milk
- ½ tablespoon raisins
- ¼ teaspoon baking powder

No-Bake Peanut Butter Protein Bites and Dark Chocolate

Preparation Time: 20 minutes + chill time, Cooking Time: nil , Servings: 10
Ingredients:
- 1 cup old fashioned rolled oats
- 1 cup vanilla protein powder
- ¾ cup smooth natural peanut butter

- 2 tablespoons ground flaxseed
- 1 tablespoon ground flaxseed
- 1 tablespoon chia seeds
- 1 teaspoon vanilla extract
- ¼ cup dark chocolate chips
- ¾ teaspoons stevia baking blend
- 1 tablespoon water

Instructions:
1. Take a bowl and mix In oats, protein powder, peanut butter, flaxseed, chia seeds, vanilla, chocolate chips, stevia, and water.
2. Let it chill for 30 minutes.
3. Roll the mixture into 25 balls, eat and enjoy!

Nutritional Value Per Serving:
Calories: 181; Total Fat: 10g; Saturated Fat: 0g; Protein: 11g; Carbs: 11g; Fiber: 3g

Hearty Overnight Oats

Preparation Time: 3 minutes + 12 hours overnight sit , Cooking Time: nil   , Servings: 4
Ingredients:
- ¾ cup Fat-Free Greek yogurt
- 2 tablespoons protein powder
- 1 and ¼ cup semi-skimmed milk

- 2 tablespoons Chia seeds
- 1 cup porridge oats

Instructions:
1. Add yogurt, protein powder, milk, chia seeds, and oats in a bowl and mix well.
2. Spoon mixture into four servings and cover them.
3. Let the mixture sit in the fridge overnight.
4. Serve by stirring the mixture and topping it with seeds, nuts, and fruits.
5. Enjoy!

Nutritional Value Per Serving:
Calories: 338 , Total Fat: 10g , Saturated Fat: 2g , Protein: 22g , Carbs: 34g, Fiber: 9g

Awesome Cheesy Grits

Preparation Time: 5 minutes , Cooking Time: 5-10 minutes, Servings: 4

Ingredients:

- 1 cup uncooked grits
- 5 whole eggs
- 1 cup cheddar cheese, shredded
- ¼ cup half and half

Instructions:

1. Prepare your grits according to the packet.
2. Take a small bowl and mix in beaten eggs and cheese.
3. Once grits are done, stir in 3 tablespoons hot grits into egg mixture.
4. Add egg mixture to the cooking grits, whisk in egg mixture into grits until smooth.
5. Add half and half, whisk until grits reach your desired consistency.
6. Enjoy!

Nutritional Value Per Serving:
Calories: 304, Total Fat: 10g, Saturated Fat: 2g , Protein: 16g, Carbs: 36g , Fiber: 6g

Fancy Vegan Porridge

Preparation Time: 5 minutes , Cooking Time: 5 minutes , Servings: 2

Ingredients:

- 2 tablespoons coconut flour
- 3 tablespoons flaxseed meal
- 2 tablespoons protein powder
- 1 and ½ cups unsweetened almond milk
- Powdered Erythritol

Instructions:

1. Take a bowl and add flaxseed, coconut flour, protein powder.
2. Take a saucepan and place it over medium heat, add almond milk and cook until the mixture starts to thicken.
3. Stir in a preferred portion of sweetener and serve with your desired topping.
4. Enjoy!

Nutritional Value Per Serving:
Calories: 112 , Total Fat: 5g, Saturated Fat: 1g, Protein: 4g , Carbs: 11g , Fiber: 4g

Pumpkin Porridge

Preparation Time: 10 minutes ,
Cooking Time: 30 minutes   ,
Servings: 3

Ingredients:

- 1 cup pumpkin, chopped
- 1 cup fresh arugula, chopped
- 3 tablespoons almonds, ground
- 1 teaspoon dry rosemary, chopped
- ½ teaspoon dry thyme, ground
- 1 tablespoon olive oil

Instructions:

1. Pre-heat your oven to 350 degrees F.
2. Peel pumpkin and cut it lengthwise in half. Scrape out seeds and one large wedge.
3. Cut into fine chunks and fill up measuring cup, wrap remaining of pumpkin in plastic foil and chill for a while.
4. Take a large baking sheet and grease with olive oil, spread pumpkin and sprinkle rosemary and thyme.
5. Bake for 30 minutes, remove from oven and let them cool.
6. Take a bowl and add arugula, ground almonds, add baked pumpkin and drizzle olive oil.
7. Stir well and enjoy!

Nutritional Value Per Serving:

Calories: 158, Total Fat: 12g ,
Saturated Fat: 2g, Protein: 5g , Carbs:
12g , Fiber: 3g

Strawberry Orange Salad

Preparation Time: 10 minutes, Cooking Time: nil, Servings: 4

Ingredients:
- 1 cup fresh strawberries, chopped
- 1 medium-sized orange, chopped
- ½ cup fresh cranberries
- 1 cup romaine lettuce, chopped
- 3 tablespoons lemon juice, squeezed
- ¼ teaspoon cinnamon, ground

Instructions:
1. Wash strawberries thoroughly and cut into bite-sized portions.
2. Add cranberries to a colander and wash under cold water, drain them.
3. Wash lettuce thoroughly and roughly chop, peel orange and divide into wedges.
4. Cut each wedge in half and keep it on the side.
5. Take a small bowl and add lemon juice, cinnamon, stir well.
6. Add strawberries, cranberries lettuce in salad bowl.
7. Drizzle dressing and serve, enjoy!

Nutritional Value Per Serving:
Calories: 79, Total Fat: 0.5g, Saturated Fat: 0g , Protein: 1.4g, Carbs: 17g, Fiber: 2g

Stage 4: Solid foods

Avocado Shrimp Salad

Preparation Time: 15 Minutes,
Servings: 4

Ingredients:
- 1 ripe avocado
- 1 tbsp Tabasco
- 1 tsp ranch dressing
- ½ cup yogurt
- 1 lb shrimp, cooked
- 1 grapefruit, cut into sections

Instructions:
1. Combine together Tabasco, ranch dressing and yogurt.
2. Place shrimp, avocado and grapefruit in large bowl.
3. Pour dressing over shrimp and avocado mixture.
4. Serve and enjoy.

Nutritional Value per Serving:
Calories: 226, Fat: 10.2 g,
Carbohydrates: 11.2 g, Sugar: 4.7 g,
Protein: 24.2 g, Cholesterol: 164 mg

Millet Congee

Preparation Time: 15 Minutes
Cook Time: 60 Minutes, Servings: 4

Ingredients:
- 1 cup millet
- 5 cups water
- 1 cup diced sweet potato
- 1 tsp. cinnamon
- 2 tbsps. stevia
- 1 diced apple
- ¼ cup honey

Instructions:
1. In a deep pot, add stevia, sweet potato, cinnamon, water and millet, then stir to combine.
2. Bring to boil over high heat, then reduce to a simmer on low for an hour or until water is fully absorbed and millet is cooked.
3. Stir in remaining ingredients and serve.

Nutritional Value per Serving:
Calories: 136, Fat: 1g, Carbs: 28.5g,
Protein: 3.1g

Easy Baked Salmon

Preparation Time: 9 Minutes, Cooking Time: 16 minutes, Servings: 4

Ingredients:
- 4 salmon fillets
- 1 lemon zest
- 1 tsp sea salt
- 3 oz olive oil
- 1 garlic clove, minced
- 1 tsp fresh dill, chopped
- 1 tbsp fresh parsley, chopped
- 1/8 tsp white pepper

Instructions:
1. Preheat the oven at 200°C.
2. Place all ingredients except salmon fillet in microwave safe bowl and microwave for 45 seconds.
3. Stir well until combine.
4. Place salmon fillets on parchment lined baking dish.
5. Spread evenly olive oil and herb mixture over each salmon fillet.
6. Place in preheated oven and bake for 15 minutes.
7. Serve and enjoy.

Nutritional Value per Serving:
Calories: 408, Fat: 30.9 g, Carbohydrates: 0.5 g, Sugar: 0 g, Protein: 34.7 g, Cholesterol: 78 mg

Berry Muesli

Preparation Time: 6 hours 10 minutes, Servings: 2

Ingredients:
- 1 cup oats
- 1 cup fruit flavored yogurt
- ½ cup milk
- 1/8 tsp. salt
- ½ cup dried raisins
- ½ cup chopped apple
- ½ cup frozen blueberries
- ¼ cup chopped walnuts

Instructions:
Combine yogurt, salt and oats together in a medium bowl, mix well, then cover the mixture tightly.
Place in the refrigerator to cool for 6 hours.
3. Add raisins, and apples the gently fold.
4. Top with walnuts and serve. Enjoy!

Nutritional Value per Serving:
Calories: 198, Carbs: 31.2g, Fat: 4.3g, Protein: 6g

Mushroom Strata and Turkey Sausage

Preparation Time: 15 Minutes, Cooking Time: 60 Minutes, Servings: 12

Ingredients:
- 8 oz. cubed ciabatta bread
- 12 oz. chopped turkey sausage
- 2 cups milk
- 4 oz. shredded cheddar
- 3 eggs
- 12 oz. egg substitute
- ½ cup chopped green onion
- 1 cup sliced mushroom
- ½ tsp. paprika
- ½ tsp. pepper
- 2 tbsps. grated parmesan cheese

Instructions:
1. Set oven to 400°F. Lay bread cubes flat on a baking tray and set it to toast for about 8 min.
2. Meanwhile, add a skillet over medium heat with sausage and allow to cook while stirring, until fully brown and crumbled.
3. In a bowl, add pepper, parmesan cheese, egg substitute, salt, paprika, eggs, cheddar cheese and milk, then whisk to combine.
4. Add in remaining ingredients and toss well to incorporate. Transfer mixture to a large baking dish (preferably a 9x13-inch) then tightly cover and allow to rest in the refrigerator overnight.
5. Set oven to 350°F, remove the cover from casserole dish and set to bake until fully cooked and golden brown.
6. Slice and serve.

Nutritional Value per Serving:
Calories: 185 , Fat: 18g , Carbohydrates: 9.2g, Protein: 2.4g

Avocado Cherry Smoothie

Preparation time: 5 minutes , Cooking Time: - , Servings: 3

Ingredients:
- ½ ripe avocado, chopped
- 1 cup fresh cherries
- 1 cup coconut water, sugar-free
- 1 whole lime

Preparation:
1. Peel the avocado and cut in half. Remove the pit and chop into bite-sized pieces. Reserve the rest in the refrigerator. Set aside.
2. Rinse the cherries under cold running water using a large colander. Cut each in half and remove the pits. Set aside.
3. Peel the lime and cut in half. Set aside.
4. Now, combine avocado, cherries, coconut water, and lime in a blender. Pulse to combine and transfer to a serving glass.
5. Add few ice cubes and refrigerate for 10 minutes before serving.

Nutrition value per serving:
Calories: 128, Protein: 1.7g, Total Carbs: 17g, Dietary Fibers: 3.8g, Total Fat: 6.8g

Strawberry & Mushroom Sandwich

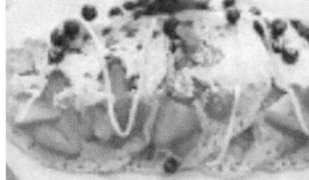

Preparation Time: 10 minutes, Servings: 4

Ingredients:
- 8 oz. Cream cheese

sp. Honey
sp. grated Lemon zest
iced Portobello Mushrooms
ip sliced Strawberries
ctions:
honey, lemon zest and cheese to a
l processor, and process until fully
orporated.
cheese mixture to spread on
hrooms as you would butter.
3. Top with strawberries. Enjoy!

Nutritional Value per Serving:
Calories: 180, Fat: 16g, Carbs: 6g, Protein: 2g

Quinoa Bowls

Preparation Time: 10 minutes
Cook Time: 25 minutes, Servings: 2
Ingredients:
- 1 sliced peach
- 1/3 cup quinoa
- 1 cup low fat milk
- ½ tsp. vanilla extract
- 2 tsps. natural stevia
- 12 raspberries
- 14 blueberries
- 2 tsps. honey

Instructions:
1. Add natural stevia, 2/3 cup milk and quinoa to a saucepan, and stir to combine.
2. Over medium high heat, bring to a boil then cover and reduce heat to a low simmer for a further 20 minutes.
3. Grease and preheat grill to medium. Grill peach slices for about a minute per side. Set aside.
4. Heat remaining milk in the microwave and set aside.
5. Split cooked quinoa evenly between 2 serving bowls and top evenly with remaining ingredients. Enjoy!

Nutritional Value per Serving:
Calories: 180, Fat: 4g, Carbs: 36g, Protein: 4.5g

Vanilla Egg Custard

Preparation Time: 10 Minutes
Cook Time: 30 Minutes, Servings: 6
Ingredients:
- 4 large eggs
- 2 tsp vanilla extract
- 2/3 cup splenda
- 12 oz can evaporated milk
- 1 cup milk
- ½ cup Nutmeg, grated

Directions:
1. Preheat the oven at 325 F.
2. Place six ramekins in baking tray and set aside.
3. Add vanilla, splenda, eggs, evaporated milk and milk in blender and blend until smooth.
4. Pour mixture into the ramekins then pour enough water in baking tray and bake in preheated oven for 30 minutes.
5. Serve chilled and enjoy.

Nutritional Value per Serving:
Calories: 255, Fat: 8.4 g,
Carbohydrates: 29.5 g, Sugar: 29.5 g,
Protein: 9.4 g, Cholesterol: 144 mg

Asparagus Omelet

Preparation Time: 7 Minutes, Cooking Time: 3 Minutes, Servings: 2
Ingredients:
- 4 asparagus spears, peel lower half
- 4 tbsp parmesan cheese, grated
- 3 large eggs
- 2 tsp olive oil
- 1 garlic clove, minced
- Pepper
- Salt

Directions:
1. Heat olive oil in pan over medium heat.
2. Add asparagus and garlic in pan and sauté for 3 minutes.
3. Whisk together eggs, cheese, 1 tbsp water, pepper and salt.
4. Pour egg mixture over the asparagus and cook until desired doneness.
5. Serve and enjoy.

Nutritional Value per Serving:
Calories: 159, Fat: 12.2 g,
Carbohydrates: 3.0 g, Sugar: 1.5 g,
Protein: 10.6 g, Cholesterol: 279 mg

Cold Tomato Couscous

Preparation time: 15 Minutes ,
Cooking Time: 7-10 Minutes,
Servings: 4

Ingredients:

- 5 oz couscous
- 3 tbsp tomato sauce
- 3 tbsp lemon juice
- 1 small-sized onion, chopped
- 1 cup vegetable stock
- ½ small-sized cucumber, sliced
- ½ small-sized carrot, sliced
- ¼ tsp salt
- 3 tbsp olive oil
- ½ cup fresh parsley, chopped

Instructions:

1. First, pour the couscous into a large bowl. Boil the vegetable broth and slightly add in the couscous while stirring constantly. Leave it for about 10 minutes until couscous absorbs the liquid. Cover with a lid and set aside. Stir from time to time to speed up the soaking process and break the lumps with a spoon.
2. Meanwhile, preheat the olive oil in a frying pan, and add the tomato sauce. Add chopped onion and stir until translucent. Set aside and let it cool for a few minutes.
3. Add the oily tomato sauce to the couscous and stir well. Now add lemon juice, chopped parsley, and salt to the mixture and give it a final stir.
4. Serve with sliced cucumber, carrot, and parsley.

Nutritional Value Per Serving:

Calories: 249, Protein: 5.6g, Total Carbs: 32.8g , Dietary Fibers: 3.2g, Total Fat: 11g

Wild Salmon Salad

Preparation time: 10 Minutes,
Servings: 2

Ingredients:

- 2 medium-sized cucumbers, sliced
- A handful of iceberg lettuce, torn
- ¼ cup sweet corn
- 1 large tomato, roughly chopped
- 8 oz smoked wild salmon, sliced
- 4 tbsp freshly squeezed orange juice

Dressing:

- 1 ¼ cup liquid yogurt, 2% fat
- 1 tbsp fresh mint, finely chopped
- 2 garlic cloves, crushed
- 1 tbsp sesame seeds

Instructions:

1. Combine vegetables in a large bowl. Drizzle with orange juice and top with salmon slices. Set aside.
2. In another bowl, whisk together yogurt, mint, crushed garlic, and sesame seeds.
3. Drizzle over salad and toss to combine. Serve cold.

Nutritional Value Per Serving:
Calories: 249 , Protein: 5.6g, Total Carbs: 32.8g, Dietary Fibers: 3.2g, Total Fat: 11g

Lean Spring Stew

Preparation time: 20 Minutes ,
Cooking Time:1 hour 15 Minutes   ,
Servings: 4

Ingredients:

- 1 lb diced fire roasted tomatoes
- 4 boneless & skinless chicken thighs
- 1 tbsp dried basil
- 8 oz chicken stock
- Salt & pepper to taste
- 4 oz tomato paste
- 3 chopped celery stalks
- 3 chopped carrots
- 2 chili peppers, finely chopped
- 2 tbsp olive oil
- 1 finely chopped onion
- 2 garlic cloves, crushed
- ½ container mushrooms
- Sour cream

Instructions:

1. Heat up the olive oil over medium-high temperature. Add the celery, onions and carrots and stir-fry for 5 to 10 minutes.
2. Transfer to a deep pot and add tomato paste, basil, garlic, mushrooms and seasoning. Keep stirring the vegetables until they are completely covered by tomato sauce. At the same time, cut the chicken into small cubes to make it easier to eat.
3. Put the chicken in a deep pot, pour the chicken stock over it and throw in the tomatoes.
4. Stir the chicken in to ensure the ingredients and vegetables are properly mixed with it. Turn the heat to low and cook for about an hour. The vegetables and chicken should be cooked through before you turn the heat off. Top with sour cream and serve!

Nutritional Value Per serving:

Calories: 277, Protein: 25.6g , Total Carbs: 19g, Dietary Fibers: 5.3g , Total Fat: 11.9g

Red Orange Salad

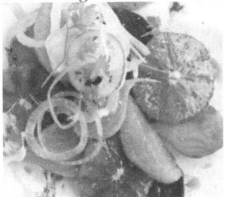

Preparation time: 15 Minutes ,
Cooking Time: 20 Minutes, Servings:
3

Ingredients:
- Fresh lettuce leaves, rinsed
- 1 small cucumber sliced
- ½ red bell pepper, sliced
- 1 cup frozen seafood mix
- 1 onion, peeled and finely chopped
- 3 garlic cloves, crushed
- ¼ cup fresh orange juice
- 5 tbsp extra virgin olive oil
- Salt to taste

Instructions:
1. Heat up 3 tbsp of extra virgin olive oil over medium-high temperature. Add chopped onion and crushed garlic. Stir fry for about 5 minutes.
2. Reduce the heat to minimum and add 1 cup of frozen seafood mix. Cover and cook for about 15 minutes, until soft. Remove from the heat and allow it to cool for a while.
3. Meanwhile, combine the vegetables in a bowl. Add the remaining 2 tbsp of olive oil, fresh orange juice and a little salt. Toss well to combine.
4. Top with seafood mix and serve immediately.

Nutritional Value Per serving:
Calories: 206, Protein: 7g, Total
Carbs: 13.1g , Dietary Fibers: 1.8g,
Total Fat: 14.6g

Fresh Shrimp Spring Rolls

Preparation Time: 20 Minutes,
Servings: 12

Ingredients:
- 12 sheets rice paper
- 12 bib lettuce
- 12 basil laves
- ¾ cup cilantro
- 1 cup shredded carrots
- ½ sliced cucumber
- 20 oz. cooked shrimp

Instructions:
1. Add all vegetables and shrimp to separate bowls.
2. Set a damp paper towel tower flat on work surface.
3. Quickly wet a sheet of rice papers under warm water and lay on paper towel.
4. Top with 1 of each vegetable and 4 pieces of shrimp, then roll in rice paper into a burrito – like roll.
5. Repeat until all vegetables and shrimp has been used up. Serve and enjoy.

Nutritional Value Per Serving:
Calories: 67, Fat: 2.9g , Carbs: 7.4g, Protein: 2.6g

Sunshine Wrap

Preparation Time: 30 Minutes,
Servings: 2

Ingredients:
- 8 oz. grilled chicken breast
- ½ cup diced celery
- 2/3 cup mandarin oranges
- ¼ cup minced onion
- 2 tbsps. mayonnaise
- 1 tsp. soy sauce
- ¼ tsp. garlic powder
- ¼ tsp. black pepper
- 1 whole wheat tortilla
- 4 lettuce leaves

Instructions:
1. Combine all ingredients, except tortilla and lettuce, in a large bowl and toss to evenly coat.
2. Lay tortillas on a flat surface and cut into quarters.
3. Top each quarter with a lettuce leaf and spoon chicken mixture into the middle of each.
4. Roll each tortilla into a cone and seal by slightly wetting the edge with water. Enjoy!

Nutritional Value Per Serving:

Calories: 280.8, Fat: 21.1g ,
Carbohydrates: 3g , Protein: 19g

Sweet Roasted Beet & Arugula Tortilla Pizza V

Preparation Time: 15 Minutes,
Cooking Time: 10 Minutes, Servings: 6
Ingredients:
- 2 chopped Beets
- 6 Corn Tortillas
- 1 c. Arugula
- ½ c. Goat cheese
- 1 c. Blackberries

- 2 tbsps. Honey
- 2 tbsps. Balsamic vinegar

Instructions:
1. Preheat oven to 350 F. Lay tortillas on a flat surface.
2. Top with beets, berries and goat cheese. Combine balsamic vinegar and honey together in a small bowl, and whisk to combine.
3. Drizzle the mixture over pizza and to bake for about 10 minutes, or until cheese has melted slightly and tortilla is crisp.
4. Garnish with arugula and serve.

Nutritional Value Per Serving:
Calories: 286 , Fat: 40g ,
Carbohydrates: 42g, Protein: 15g

Mayo-less Tuna Salad

Preparation Time: 5 Minutes,
Servings: 2
Ingredients:
- 5 oz. tuna
- 1 tbsp. olive oil

- 1 tbsp. red wine vinegar
- ¼ cup chopped green onion
- 2 cup arugula
- 1 cup cooked pasta
- 1 tbsp. parmesan cheese
- Black pepper

Instructions:
1. Combine all ingredients into a medium bowl. Split mixture between two plates. Serve, and enjoy.

Nutritional Value Per Serving:
Calories: 213.2, Fat: 6.2g,
Carbohydrates: 20.3g, Protein: 22.7g

Southwestern Black Bean Cakes with Guacamole

Preparation Time: 15 Minutes,
Cooking Time: 10 Minutes, Servings: 4

Ingredients:
- 1 cup whole wheat bread crumbs
- 3 tbsps. chopped cilantro
- 2 garlic cloves
- 15 oz. black beans
- 7 oz. chipotle peppers in adobo sauce
- 1 tsp. ground cumin
- 1 large egg
- ½ diced avocado
- 1 tbsp. lime juice
- 1 tomato plum

Instructions:
1. Drain beans and add all ingredients, except avocado, lime juice and eggs, to a food processor and run until the mixture begins to pull away from the sides.
2. Transfer to a large bowl and add egg, then mix well.
3. Form into 4 even patties and cook on a preheated, greased grill over medium heat for about 10 minutes, flipping halfway through.
4. Add avocado and lime juice in a small bowl, then stir and mash together using a fork.
5. Season to taste then serve with bean cakes.

Nutritional Value Per Serving:
Calories: 178 , Fat: 7g , Carbohydrates: 25g , Protein: 11g

Southwest Style Zucchini Rice Bowl

Preparation Time: 12 Minutes, Servings: 2

Ingredients:
- 1 tbsp. vegetable oil
- 1 cup chopped vegetables
- 1 cup chopped chicken breast
- 1 cup cooked zucchini rice
- 4 tbsps. salsa
- 2 tbsps. shredded cheddar cheese
- 2 tbsps. sour cream

Instructions:
1. Set a skillet with oil to heat up over medium heat.
2. Add chopped vegetables and allow to cook, stirring until vegetables become fork tender.
3. Add chicken and zucchini rice. Cook while stirring, until fully heated through.
4. Split between 2 serving bowls and garnish with remaining ingredients. Serve and enjoy!

Nutritional Value Per Serving:
Calories: 168, Fat: 8.2g ,
Carbohydrates: 18g , Protein: 5.5g

Tandoori Chicken

Preparation Time: 7 Minutes, Cooking Time:30 Minutes, Servings: 6

Ingredients:

- 1 cup plain yogurt
- ½ cup lemon juice
- 5 crushed garlic cloves
- 2 tbsps. paprika
- 1 tsp. yellow curry powder
- 1 tsp. ground ginger
- 6 skinless chicken breasts
- 6 skewers

Instructions:

1. Set oven to 400 degrees F. In blender, combine red pepper flakes, ginger, curry, paprika, garlic, lemon juice and yogurt, then process into a smooth paste.
2. Add chicken strips evenly onto skewers. Add chicken to a shallow casserole dish then cover with ½ of yogurt mixture.
3. Tightly seal and rest in refrigerator for about 15 minutes.
4. Lightly grease a baking tray, then transfer chicken skewers onto it, and top with remaining yogurt mixture.
5. Set to bake until the chicken is fully cooked. Serve and enjoy.

Nutritional Value Per Serving:

Calories: 177, Fat: 7.2g, Carbs: 6g , Protein: 20.6g

Turkey Fajitas Bowls

Preparation Time: 10 Minutes,
Cooking Time: 10 Minutes, Servings: 4
Ingredients:
- ½ lb. turkey breast
- 2 tbsps. olive oil
- 1 tbsp. lemon juice
- 1 crushed garlic
- ¾ tsp. chopped chili pepper
- ½ tsp. dried oregano
- 1 sliced bell pepper
- 1 medium tomato
- ½ cup shredded cheddar cheese
- 4 tostada bowls
- 4 tbsps. salsa

Instructions:
1. Add oregano, chili pepper, garlic, lemon juice and 1tbsp. olive oil to a medium bowl. Whisk to combine.
2. Add turkey then toss to coat. Allow to marinate for about 30 min.
3. Set a skillet over medium heat with remaining oil. Add bell pepper and allow to cook for 2 minutes, stirring.
4. Add turkey and cook for 3 more minutes. Add tomato, stir and remove from heat.
5. Spoon mixture evenly into tostada bowls.
6. Garnish with cheese and salsa then serve.

Nutritional Value Per Serving:
Calories: 240, Fat: 15g, Carbs: 5g , Protein: 23g

Skinny Chicken Pesto Bake

Preparation Time: 10 Minutes,
Cooking Time: 25 Minutes, Servings: 4

Ingredients:

- 160 oz. skinless chicken
- 1 tsps. basil
- 1 sliced tomato
- 6 tbsps. shredded mozzarella cheese
- 2 tsps. grated parmesan cheese

Instructions:

1. Cut chicken into thin strips.
2. Set oven to 400 degrees F. Prepare a baking sheet by lining with parchment paper.
3. Lay chicken strips on prepared baking sheet. Top with pesto and brush evenly over chicken pieces.
4. Set to bake until chicken is fully cooked (about 15 minutes).
5. Garnish with parmesan cheese, mozzarella, and tomatoes.
6. Set to continue baking until cheese melts (about 5 minutes).

Nutritional Value Per Serving:
Calories: 205 , Fat: 8.5g , Carbs: 2.5g, Protein: 30g

Spaghetti Squash Lasagna

Preparation Time: 10 Minutes,
Cooking Time: 30 Minutes, Servings: 6

Ingredients:

- 2 cup marinara sauce
- 3 cup roasted spaghetti squash
- 1 cup ricotta
- 8 tsps. grated parmesan cheese
- 6 oz. shredded mozzarella cheese
- ¼ tsp. red pepper flakes

Instructions:

1. Set oven to preheat oven to 375 degrees F and spoon half of marinara sauce into baking dish.
2. Top with squash, then layer remaining ingredients.
3. Cover and set to bake until cheese is melted and edges brown (about 20 minutes).
4. Remove cover and return to bake for another 5 minutes. Enjoy!

Nutritional Value Per Serving:
Calories: 255, Fat: 15.9g , Carbs: 5.5g, Protein: 21.4g

Crab Mushrooms

Preparation Time: 10 Minutes,
Cooking Time: 30 Minutes, Servings:
6

Ingredients:

- 5 oz. crab meat
- 5 oz. white mushrooms
- ½ tsp. salt
- ¼ cup fish stock
- 1 tsp. butter
- ¼ tsp. ground coriander
- 1 tsp. dried cilantro
- 1 tsp. butter

Instructions:

1. Chop the crab meat and sprinkle with salt and dried cilantro.
2. Mix the crab meat carefully. Preheat the air fryer to 400 F.
3. Chop the white mushrooms and combine with crab meat.
4. Add fish stock, ground coriander and butter.
5. Transfer the side dish mixture into the air fryer basket tray.
6. Stir gently with the help of a plastic spatula.
7. Cook the side dish for 5 minutes.
8. Rest for 5 minutes.   Serve and enjoy!

Nutritional Value Per Serving:
Calories: 56 , Fat: 1.7g ,
Carbohydrates: 2.6g, Protein: 7g

Loaded Sweet Potatoes

Preparation Time: 10 Minutes, Cooking Time: 30 Minutes, Servings: 6

Ingredients:
- 4 medium sweet potatoes, baked
- ½ cup Greek yogurt
- 1 tsp. taco seasoning
- 1 tsp. olive oil
- 1 diced red pepper
- ½ diced red onion
- 1 1/3 cup canned black beans
- ½ cup Mexican cheese blend
- ¼ cup chopped cilantro
- ½ cup salsa

Instructions:
1. Mix taco seasoning and yogurt well, then set aside.
2. Set a skillet over medium heat with oil to get hot.
3. Add in remaining ingredients, except potatoes, cheese and salsa, and cook for about 8 minutes or until fully heated through.
4. Slightly pierce potatoes down the center and top evenly with all remaining ingredients. Serve.

Nutritional Value Per Serving:
Calories: 311 , Fat: 8.3g , Carbohydrates: 57g , Protein: 3.2g

Cherry Tomatoes Tilapia Salad

Preparation Time: 7 Minutes, Cooking Time: 18 Minutes, Servings: 3

Ingredients:
- 1 cup mixed greens
- 1 cup cherry tomatoes
- 1/3 cup diced red onion
- 1 medium avocado
- 3 tortilla crusted tilapia fillet

Instructions:
1. Spray tilapia fillet with a little bit of cooking spray. Put fillets in air fryer basket. Cook for 18 minutes at about 390° F.
2. Transfer the fillet to a bowl. Toss with tomatoes, greens and red onion. Add the lime dressing and mix again.
3. Serve and enjoy!

Nutritional Value Per Serving:
Calories: 271, Fat: 8g , Carbohydrates: 10.1g, Protein: 18.5g

Coconut Flour Spinach Casserole

Preparation Time: 10 minutes, Cooking Time: 30 minutes, Servings: 6

Ingredients:

- 4 eggs
- ¾ cup unsweetened almond milk
- 3 oz. chopped spinach
- 3 oz. chopped artichoke hearts
- 1 cup grated parmesan
- 3 minced garlic cloves
- 1 tsp. salt
- ½ tsp. pepper
- ¾ c. coconut flour
- 1 tbsp. baking powder

Instructions:

1. Preheat air fryer to 375 degrees F. Grease air fryer pan with cooking spray.
2. Whisk eggs with almond milk, spinach, artichoke hearts and ½ cup of parmesan cheese. Add salt, garlic and pepper.
3. Add the coconut flour and baking powder; whisk until well combined.
4. Spread mixture into air fryer pan and sprinkle remaining cheese over it.
5. Place the baking pan in the air fryer and cook for about 30 minutes.
6. Remove baking pan from air fryer and sprinkle with chopped basil. Slice, then serve and enjoy!

Nutritional Value Per Serving:
Calories: 175.2, Fat: 10.3g, Carbohydrates: 2.4g, Protein: 17.7g

Strawberry Frozen Yogurt Squares

Preparation Time: 8 Hours, Servings: 8

Ingredients:
- 1 cup barley & wheat cereal
- 3 cup fat-free strawberry yogurt
- 10 oz. frozen strawberries
- 1 cup fat- free milk
- 1 cup whipped topping

Instructions:
1. Set a parchment paper on the baking tray.
2. Spread cereal evenly over the bottom of the tray.
3. Add milk, strawberries and yogurt to blender, and process into a smooth mixture.
4. Use yogurt mixture to top cereal, wrap with foil, and place to freeze until firm (about 8 hours).
5. Slightly thaw, slice into squares and serve.

Nutritional Value Per Serving:
Calories: 188, Fat: 0g,, Carbs: 43.4g , Protein: 4.6g

Smoked Tofu Quesadillas

Preparation Time: 20 Minutes, Cooking Time: 5 Minutes, Servings: 4

Ingredients:
- 1 lb. extra firm sliced tofu
- 12 tortillas
- 2 tbsps. coconut oil
- 6 slices cheddar cheese
- 2 tbsps. sundried tomatoes
- 1 tbsp. cilantro
- 5 tbsps. sour cream

Instructions:
1. Lay one tortilla flat and fill with tofu, tomato, cheese and top with oil. Repeat for as many as you need.
2. Bake for 5 minutes and remove from flame.
3. Top with sour cream.

Nutritional Value Per Serving:
Calories: 136 , Fat: 6g , Carbs: 13g , Protein: 10g

Zucchini Pizza Boats

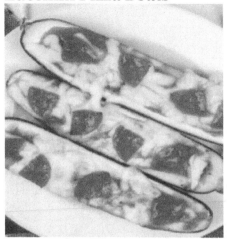

Preparation Time: 15 Minutes, Cooking Time: 30 Minutes, Servings: 2

Ingredients:
- 2 medium Zucchini
- ½ cup Tomato Sauce
- ½ cup shredded Mozzarella cheese
- 2 tbsps. Parmesan cheese

Instructions:
1. Set oven to 350 degrees F.
2. Slice zucchini in half lengthwise and spoon out the core and seeds to form boats.
3. Place zucchini halves skin side down in a small baking dish.
4. Add remaining ingredients inside the hollow center then set to bake until golden brown and fork tender (about 30 minutes).
5. Serve and enjoy.

Nutritional Value Per Serving:
Calories: 214 , Fat: 7.9g , Carbs: 23.6g, Protein: 15.2g

Pear-Cranberry Pie with Oatmeal Streusel

Preparation Time: 30 Minutes, Cooking Time: 1 Hour, Servings: 6

Ingredients:
Streusel:
- ¾ cup oats
- 1/3 cup stevia
- ½ tsp. cinnamon
- ¼ tsp. nutmeg
- 1 tbsp. cubed butter

Filling:
- 3 cup cubed pears
- 2 cup cranberries
- ½ cup stevia
- 2½ tbsps. cornstarch

Instructions:
1. Set oven to 350 degrees F.
2. Combine all streusel ingredients in a food processor and process into a coarse crumb.
3. Next, combine all filling ingredients in a large bowl and toss to combine.
4. Transfer filling into pie crust, then top with streusel mix.
5. Set to bake until golden brown (about an hour). Cool and serve.

Nutritional Value Per Serving:
Calories: 280 , Fat: 9g , Carbs: 47g, Protein: 1g

Macerated Summer Berries with Frozen Yogurt

Preparation Time: 2 Hours, Servings: 4

Ingredients:
- 1 cup sliced strawberries
- 1 cup blueberries
- 1 cup raspberries
- 1 tbsp. stevia
- 1 tsp. orange zest
- 2 tbsps. orange juice
- 1-pint low fat yogurt

Instructions:
1. Add stevia, orange zest, orange juice and berries to a large bowl.
2. Toss to combine. Set to chill for at least 2 hours.
3. Divide yogurt evenly into 4 serving bowls, top evenly with berry mixture and serve.

Nutritional Value Per Serving:
Calories: 133 , Fat: 1g, Carbs: 28.4g, Protein: 1.3g

Pumpkin Pie Spiced Yogurt

Preparation Time: 10 Minutes, Cooking Time: 5 Minutes, Servings: 2

Ingredients:
- 2 cup low fat plain yogurt
- ½ cup pumpkin puree
- ¼ tsp. cinnamon
- ¼ tsp. pumpkin pie spice
- ¼ cup chopped walnuts
- 1 tbsp. honey

Instructions:
1. Combine spices with the pumpkin puree in a medium bowl and stir.
2. Stir in yogurt, divide into 2 serving glasses. Top with honey and walnuts. Serve and enjoy!

Nutritional Value Per Serving:
Calories: 208 , Fat: 7g , Carbs: 22g, Protein: 16g

Chocolate Ice Cream

Preparation Time: 1 Hour, Cooking Time:, Servings: 8

Ingredients

- 4 4oz vanilla and chocolate yogurt
- 2/3 cup low-fat custard
- 2 tbsp. low-fat hot chocolate powder
- 2 scoops flavorless protein powder
- 2/3 cup skim milk

Instructions

1. Mix the yogurt, chocolate powder, protein powder, milk, and custard together.
2. Pour the mixture into a freezer safe bowl and allow it to freeze until it has completely firmed up. Whisk the mixture every 30 minutes. This will ensure that large ice crystals don't form and it has more of an ice cream consistency. If you have an ice cream maker, you can place the mixture into it and mix before you place it in the freezer.
3. Before you serve, you should let it set for around 30 minutes to soften just a bit.

Nutritional Value Per Serving:

Calories: 352, Sodium: 111mg, Cholesterol: 161mg, Protein: 4g, Carbohydrates: 26.9g, Fat: 26.7g

Conclusion

I have covered most of the issues related to sleeve gastrectomy in this cookbook, which will work like a handbook, who are planning for bariatric surgery. Also, I hope the cookbook will guide you to lead a healthy life, without having any worries of what to eat, and what portion to consume after sleeve gastrectomy. Do contact me for any information on bariatric surgery and post-surgery diet plan and also write to me if any shortfalls or suggestions about the cookbook.

Made in the USA
Monee, IL
04 December 2019

17930020R00052